FOREWORD

New homes have gotten larger and larger over the last few decades, but lately there has been something of a turnaround, a growing appreciation of the smaller, more modest abode. Many agree, an outsized house just doesn't quite have the cozy, homey feel you find in a dwelling with less expansive square footage.

If you have a petite home or apartment, appreciate its comforting qualities, even as you contemplate the one downside universal to all smaller spaces: lack of storage. Families with diverse interests need places to put equipment, collectibles and accessories, so those with limited closet and cupboard space are always on the look-out for new storage solutions.

This book is for you if you're looking for easy storage ideas to put to use in the kitchen, living/family rooms, bathrooms, office, virtually every room in the house. *Small Space Survival Guide* is filled with tips for making the most of the square footage you have by reducing clutter and keeping everything organized and easy to find.

Most of the solutions in these pages are quick fixes that won't strain your budget or your back. Items you can find in local stores are put to use in new and interesting ways, many which put an emphasis on decorative appeal as well as organization. Some ideas are temporary, such as for a college dorm room, while others can become a permanent asset and a boon to your home's resale value.

Also included inside are three true success stories featuring people who have done wonderful things with their own "small spaces." Read about how a bachelor, small business owners and three coeds learned to survive and thrive in small spaces that they've come to truly love.

TABLE OF CONTENTS

DRESSING UP THE DORM

The toughest decorating challenge for students, Corinne Carey, Jayme Ashlock and Jenny Shai, living in the new dorms at Cal State San Marcos is not paying for the décor they want, it's hanging their coveted posters, photos, mirrors and bulletin boards on their walls and from their windows without the benefit of a hammer and nails.

"You can't put nails in. You can only use pushpins," explains a freshman student. She and her three roommates are all living away from home for the first time. They share a 1,100 square foot furnished apartment. To make their decorating ideas a reality in this home away from home, students need creative flair and an equal measure of ingenuity.

The rules for this apartment are no different from most dorms or college apartments. Students are expected to leave their rooms as they found them, so no nails or screws in the walls, no painting or wallpapering. Students are free to do whatever decorating they like in the rooms as long as they follow the policies and procedures.

The first decorating challenge for these freshman roommates was affixing without nails, a 9-foot poster of a shirtless male model on the living room wall (1). The poster boy was nicknamed Kyle by the roommates. Kyle was ultimately push-pinned into place and became the focal point for their shared living room. Before further decorating, the girls together spent $600 at various discount and linen stores on such items as a side table and lamp, candle holders, dartboard, egg-ball lamp, place mats, napkins and napkin rings, shower curtains, dinner-ware, and a bulletin board.

The living room window treatment (2) was their best deal. They bought velvety tasseled valances for $1.40 each from a linen outlet's closing sale. Relying on pushpins again, they hung the four valances across the living room window and accented them with a string of novelty lights.

Their bulletin board hangs precariously on the wall in their kitchen. "If we even touch it, it will fall," one of the students remarked.

Dartboards are popular items, but without nails, the girls are stuck with a dartboard as a table accessory.

Four male roommates share the same dartboard problem. Theirs is also, for now, an oversized coaster.

These male roommates have invested their living room with style without spending a lot of money. They bought strings of plastic beads in Day-Glo blue and yellow and hung them between the apartment's front hall and living room, dangling in front of a mini pool table. On the walls, glow-in-the-dark stars come out at night, along with a strobe light, black light, siren and even a fog machine. The evening light show is created by an accumulation of lights and lava lamps that each man brought from home.

One bedroom window stands out for its clever window treatment (3). To suspend the curtain rod without pounding nails, they zip-tied it to the top of the venetian blinds. The curtain rod looks like heavy wrought iron, but it's actually lightweight plastic. Black and beige fern-patterned fabric is draped over the rod and around the window. A special hanging mirror with hooks fits easily over a door top.

Creating a bedroom that reminds them of their home bedrooms is a goal shared by the female roommates. One has decorated with a black comforter and dark pink pillows, fuzzy pink area rug, pink scarf draped over pink storage shelves and pink throw blankets. She bought a brightly colored TV tray for $12 that she uses as a side table and a $20 floor lamp that adds color with its six bendable lamps in bright colors (4).

Another student with a goal of recreating her home bedroom has a yoga blanket on one wall with posters from home covering the other walls. A large area rug, lamps and all bed linens are new.

A large shelving unit holds photos, a stereo and mementos from home. A $20 fuzzy orange area rug is the most expensive thing purchased. Across from the shelf at the foot of the bed is an apartment fridge. A real must for keeping soft drinks and snacks cold and close-by.

See Chapter 7 starting on page 59 for more dorm room ideas.

WE ASKED MICHAEL PAYNE.

We recently had the pleasure of meeting Michael Payne, popular host of HGTV's *Designing for the Sexes*. We asked him if he had any advice for living in a very small space. He told us an amusing story about designing his dorm room when he was in college in England (believe it or not, he majored in math and physics!).

He said he had the most elegantly decorated dorm room in his college.

Since the students weren't allowed to do anything at all to their walls—no nails, paint, pictures or anything, Michael decided to add color and drama to his room anyway. He purchased several yards of indigo blue fabric that was 60" wide and painstakingly thumb-tacked it to the wall, inserting the tacks just where the wall meets the ceiling and again at the floor. Then pinned notes, quotes, pictures and mementos to the fabric.

He said his indigo blue, fabric-covered walls transformed his dreary little dorm room into a beautifully decorated space.

THE TINIEST SHOP

Who says you need lots of space to open a retail shop? Patsy Needham, Irene Christian and Jodi Snyder of Fallbrook, California, decided to think small but plan big when they rented this diminutive space for their new venture, a shop patterned after a Parisian street market.

Called *Yesterday's Garden Basket*, this shop sells gifts centered around the avocado (Fallbrook's number one product). They also self-publish their own cookbooks in the closet-size back room of the store.

This closet which measures 4' x 11' is crammed full of everything they need to produce the books, note cards and promotional mailers: a desk (actually a tabletop) and stool, two printers, a binding machine, paper cutter, scanner and two lap top computers. A drop leaf table with a chair provides more work space, while paper supplies for the books are stored neatly in divided shelves under the counter.

Scrupulous about maximizing every square inch of space, these wise ladies decided to go vertical with shelves completely covering the walls from desk to ceiling. It's here that they store excess inventory, bottled water, cleaning supplies and packing and shipping materials.

And since these busy retailers can't get away for lunch, they also fit into this mix a small refrigerator and a microwave oven.

So they don't get claustrophobic, they've stenciled a trompe l'oeil window on one wall with a French market-inspired awning. On another wall stenciled hens camouflage a electrical panel which gives a sense of dimension and adds a touch of joie de vivre.

The main part of the store which measures 4' x 13' is devoted to artificial fruits and vegetables, gift baskets, toiletries and cosmetics, avocado accessories and, of course, their avocado cook book.

These ladies certainly get our vote as retailer small space survivors!

Viewing their store proves that every square inch of space in a room can be put to work. Many of these ideas can be incorporated into a home environment: converting a closet to a home office, the use of a drop leaf table, a faux window in a claustrophobic room, and vertical shelving.

Patsy, Irene and Jodi–you're really small space inspirations.

225 SQ. FT. BACHELOR PAD

photo by Mel Melcon

Step into Bryce Prunty's condo in Santa Monica, California and enter a Tom Thumb world. Tiny dining table, mini-appliances, one closet. No pantry, no counters, no clutter.

"It's a challenge living in this small space." Prunty said of his two story, 225-square-foot unit—about half the size of a typical two-car garage. "It's a challenge, but it's fun too."

Prunty bought his one-bedroom condo for $230,000—or $1,022 a square foot—about a year ago, the day it came on the market. The condo, one of 14 converted apartments making up his complex, suits Prunty's ordered lifestyle.

"Americans are such packrats," Prunty said. "I box things I don't need. If I haven't opened the box in one year, I toss it."

His philosophy explains the lack of clutter. A pull-down storage bin, discreetly hidden behind the front door, stores his shoes, laundry and sundry items, and a free-standing butcher block stores knives, canned foods and a blender.

A wood-framed spare bed, with built-in storage drawers beneath a pale green, velvet covered mattress, is tucked beneath a small staircase that leads to the upper-level bedroom-living room. A narrow full-length mirror across from the unit's one small closet downstairs is attached to the wall with a 4-inch rod, which also provides hanging space for clothes.

Cleverly placed storage racks hold food items and cooking utensils, and Prunty has devised a tidy method for cooking dinner for his girlfriend, who frequents the cozy condo on weekends. "I clean the dishes while I cook, Prunty said. "It's a habit you get used to."

CHAPTER ONE

LIVING ROOMS / DINING ROOMS

LIVING ROOMS/ DINING ROOMS

Your living room has to be one of the most flexible rooms in your house. If you have a really small house, you have to make the very most with what you have. Here's where to start:

1. Think what you want the space to contain. Then prioritize. Do you want comfortable furniture, extra storage, an entertainment area, guest quarters, home office, place for collections or dining space?

2. Draw a floor plan of the space. Add these items from most important to least important according to your list. Does everything fit? If not, perhaps the home office, for instance, is going to have to be relegated to a spot in a hallway or bedroom.

3. Decide how much of what you already have will fit into this plan.

4. Get rid of any unneeded items.

5. Go shopping for what you need: bookcases, shelves, furniture. Check out furniture stores, home improvement centers, mail order catalogs, even thrift shops. When you have everything you need, start putting it together.

Here's some examples...

In a small living or family room that gets a lot of steady use, clutter is enemy number one! Objects piled up and strewn about only call additional attention to a lack of elbow room.

The room pictured here is quite small, but every square inch is used to best advantage with the help of built-in furnishings. Side by side shelving units hold a television and videos, books and display items, while a window seat provides extra seating with a roomy storage bin beneath. Extra blankets and throws, games or just about anything that needs to be tucked away fits inside when the cushioned seat is raised.

The cushion and pillows for this built-in window seat were hand-made to coordinate with the furniture in the room, helping to create a sense of flow that makes the room seem more spacious.

This petite living room appears quite roomy from the adjacent dining room, thanks to the open, arched entry and decorative details. The curtains are hung well above the windows, drawing the eye up toward the high ceiling, and kept to the side so the view extends to the open spaces outdoors. Note the coffee table used here, which includes drawers and a shelf for storage.

The formal dining area is adjacent to the living room pictured above. The two spaces are unified with coordinating chair cushions. The living room is visible from the dining area via an archway. This type of open floor plan will always make a small home seem larger. Slipper chairs have been brought in from the living area to provide extra seating which gives the room a fashionable eclectic style.

If your floor plan offers one rectangular room to use as a living/formal dining area, your décor can help you create a sense of two separate dwelling spaces. The borders of this cozy living room are defined by an area rug, along with matching window treatments placed high above. The valance emphasizes the height of the windows, while leaving plenty of open glass to cultivate an airy feel. Note the ottoman here, which performs double duty, providing extra seating and opening up to offer storage for a throw, magazines, etc.

The furniture in the adjacent dining room makes the most of the available space. Notice the only solid pieces in the room are the chairs at the heads of the table. The dining table is clear glass and the barstools and side chairs are open and airy, so there are few visual barriers to a view from one end of the home to the other. The cushions on both the chairs and stools coordinate with living room colors to tie the two areas together beautifully.

Placed between the living and dining rooms, this bamboo divider helps define a border without interfering with the open feeling of the cottage's floor plan (below). It doesn't block the ocean view framed by the far window, as would a screen divider or other solid piece, and it also provides shelf space for several display items. Choose furniture carefully, and you can greatly optimize your square footage!

Does a large piece of furniture have a place in a diminutive dwelling? Yes! If it's beautiful and functional, a large object provides a focal point and can add drama to a room. The armoire in this tiny beach cottage anchors the room and holds entertainment equipment, games and bed linens to use with the adjacent, pull-out sleeper sofa. An armoire is a great investment, offering a wonderful storage option for almost any room in the house.

When space in the family room is at a premium, organization and storage are a necessity! Don't be afraid to use all available wall space on one side of the room, creating a side-by-side line up of inexpensive shelf and cabinet units to hold all the playthings: everything from books, media equipment and display items to kids' games/toys and extra linens for a fold-out couch. The photograph (at left) shows you how to take advantage of all nooks and crannies, with storage baskets placed above and below cabinets and shelves lining the wall above the television.

Take advantage of every nook and architectural detail of your abode, and create some cozy little dwellings of your own. The space beneath a staircase (at right) is often used as a closet, but here it becomes a little telephone "booth." The phone and a few decorator items sit atop a small cupboard, which can store address and phone books along with notepads and pens. Beside the cupboard is a cushioned bench seat, just the place to curl up for a long chat.

A rectangular depression in the wall might be used for shelving, or you can create a charming little nook for a child. At left, decorative fabric pillows make the painted bench seat comfortable, while a bright overhead spotlight allows for illuminated reading and imaginative play. Wicker baskets below store books and toys, and a small shelf displays the child's treasures.

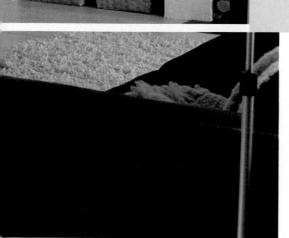

SMALL SPACE SOLUTIONS

• Find hidden spots in your home that can be transformed into functional areas like the ones pictured on this page. A niche can become a small library or a closet can can contain a home office.
• If you have odd niches here and there, add glass shelves and fill them with a prized collection.

This dining room table shows off a surprise. Covered in fabric to match the nearby sofa pillows, a piano bench replaces the fourth chair. This unique seating option can accommodate an extra guest, and ties the table in with the living room.

If you have a small kitchen with a countertop for casual dining, keep the view open by using stools without high backs. These are sturdy and comfortable looking, and they keep a low profile so as not to add visual clutter to the small space.

SMALL SPACE SOLUTIONS

• For a small room, mirrors can be used to widen and heighten a space, while intensifying the lighting.

• Hanging a mirror on the entire wall of a dining room can make that room seem twice its size. If you put the table right against the mirrored wall, your table will look twice as long.

A collection of metal tins (top right) or similar items can be decorative and offer a storage solution at the same time. A shelf full of these tins might hold office pens, paper clips and pushpins or store thread and notions in a sewing room. If you're lucky enough to have an art or craft studio, this idea could also help organize creative supplies.

Here's a unique idea for a side table. Use a smart-looking clothes hamper (below right) and you've got a great storage solution as well. This piece is the perfect size and shape to sit beside a sofa in a living or family room, and what do you know? It actually manages to evoke a casual/chic decorative mood! Lift the lid and you have lots of room for extra bedding, seasonal clothes storage or a few warming throws.

The newest coffee table designs (below) offer creative storage spaces so they're a great option for a room that's less than amply sized. This table features two rows of cubby holes, some accessorized with casually chic, wicker baskets. These compartments might hold small toys, magazines, folded throws or audio/video controls. The end result just might be a tabletop that's neat and clutter-free!

This studio apartment functions as an eating/sitting and sleeping area. Here's a way to give the illusion of divided rooms without actually screening off any of the sections. Beaded curtains create a see-through border that provides a faux barrier, one that is easily maneuvered and moved aside for entry and exit. Notice the handy chopping block/drop leaf table/storage drawers and hideaway stools all in one neat and tidy unit. The comfy couch on the other side of the curtain is actually a sleeper sofa that can be opened up at night and the living area becomes a bedroom.

SMALL SPACE SOLUTIONS

Choose furniture with dual functions:
• A sofa that makes into a bed
• A trunk as coffee table/storage container
• A drop leaf dining table/desk
• A sofa table/dining table
• Ottoman for resting feet or extra seating

This same versatile room is shown in a more romantic setting. Candles are set on the "dining" table along with a goblet of wine waiting for a gourmet dish to appear from the kitchen. Here, a colorful curtain of sheer ribbon strips divides the two areas. This panel was purchased at an import store, but it could easily be reproduced by sewing strips of wide organza ribbon to a fabric casing. Then hang on a curtain rod fastened to the ceiling.

MORE DIVIDER IDEAS

Use dividers to delineate a space. For instance, if you have a kitchen and dining area in one room, use a divider between the two. Here are some things that can be used as dividers:

• Shoji screen
• Fabric panels
• Shutters
• Beaded curtain
• Armoire
• Bookcases placed back to back
• A vintage window or door
• A row of potted plants
• An assortment of bird cages

SMALL SPACE DECORATOR TIP

Area rugs are an excellent choice when you want to define an area (see page 12). Use an area rug to delineate the following:

• a home office in the living room
• a nursery area in parent's bedroom
• craft room in the guest room
• breakfast nook in the kitchen

This cottage has a very small dining room, but the harmonizing décor makes it a stand-out. Bright yellow paint makes the room pop, and coordinates with two fabric prints that mix and match on the windows, chair cushions—even the chandelier shades. The white table and hutch are on the small side, in keeping with the proportions of the available space. The corner hutch holds serving dishes, linens and silverware, while displaying china that coordinates with the fabrics.

Many two-story houses have a landing at the top of the stairs, a small corner or loft that seems to have great potential, but for what? One idea is to place a little dining table and chairs in this space, creating an uplifted getaway for morning coffee, or just a special eating area near a guest suite. If the kids rooms are nearby, this can be a place for a quartet of friends to enjoy an afternoon snack or maybe get some homework done. If your house doesn't have a formal dining room, an upstairs nook could be a unique place to entertain guests.

This clever dinette set lets you create an informal eating area in a kitchen where there seems to be no space for one. The tiny table attaches to a wall with a folding arm that allows it to drop down and lie flat, and the skinny chairs collapse for easy storage in a nearby closet. This set would also make a great little homework station or a place to work on a laptop computer. The small shelf on the wall eliminates clutter from the table and keeps condiments close at hand.

CHAPTER TWO

KITCHENS

KITCHENS

The kitchen is often called the heart of the home. It's where food is prepared, sometimes it's a dining area, homework center or an office. It has to perform a lot of functions and if it's a small room, it's doubly important that it be organized and free of clutter.

To do this:
1. Make a floor plan of your kitchen. Draw in all the features including cupboards, stove, refrigerator, microwave, sink, dishwasher, etc.

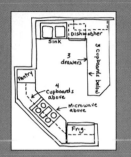

2. List the items you want to store

utensils	pots and pans
baking supplies	canned food
staples	cookbooks
linens	small appliances
cleaning supplies	dishes and glasses
wine and other spirits	pet food and supplies
appliance manuals	extension cords
tools	vases
guarantees	warranties

These cubes and drawers pictured below provide a multitude of storage solutions for a busy kitchen. They can be combined and used in countless ways. You can purchase as few or as many of them as you want to create your own "custom cabinets." See how these cubes can be used in other rooms on pages 44, 51, 65 and 69.

22

3. When going through the things in your cupboards, ask yourself these three questions, "does it work, is it easy to clean, have you used it in the last year?"

If your answer is no to any of these questions, then it's time to purge those items. Get rid of the crockpot that doesn't have a removable pan, the sandwich maker you ordered from an infomercial, the salad shooter that was a birthday gift.

4. Then ask yourself, "where do you want to store what's left?" Do you have enough cupboards and drawers for all the items you want to store?

5. If the answer is no, it's time to go shopping. Search for additional storage items, baskets or other containers to store cooking utensils, racks to hang on the wall or from the ceiling, free standing racks or cubes that can be used for extra storage.

6. Once you've drawn your plan, purchased additional storage containers, gotten rid of excess "junk", it's time to put everything away and congratulate yourself on your beautiful, new "organized kitchen."

Baskets are popular storage containers. Not only are they attractive, but they're also quite sturdy. So many storage baskets are available, some with fabric liners in solids and prints. The baskets pictured here have been spiffed up with the addition of stamped dots and handsome checked ribbon.

Whether in the kitchen, bathroom or bedroom, if the problem is storage, a versatile baker's rack can be a terrific solution. With two roomy sections on the bottom, a top shelf, wooden countertop and lots of places for hanging things, it's amazing how much you can store and organize on this piece. This versatility is illustrated in the photos on pages 24 and 26. See it also used in a bathroom setting (page 37) and a baby's room (page 45).

Placed against a wall near the kitchen table, this baker's rack holds a spice cupboard, canisters, utensils, drying herbs and baskets full of foodstuffs and baking pans. It's not only very functional, but makes a charming visual statement, especially with colorful linens draped over the basket edges. If counter space is a problem, you can opt to keep the chopping block free and available for cooking chores.

If your kitchen consists of a tiny corner in a studio apartment, the right storage pieces help you get the most of every square inch. Here, stackable cubes in your choice of shelves, drawers and open cupboards hold dishes, linens and flatware, as well as potatoes and onions in linen-lined baskets. An elevated stairstep piece is perfect for spices, while a two-tiered lazy susan puts a spin on tea supplies.

A versatile wooden table holds a microwave and offers two drawers for more storage, as well as a hiding place for a slide-away stool. Wine bottles are creatively stored in an inexpensive divided cabinet originally meant for shoes. It also nicely divides the space into a kitchen area and living/sleeping area.

SMALL SPACE SOLUTIONS

• Purchase fold-down racks or drawers that can be mounted under the cabinets.

• Buy wire racks for your cupboards for dinnerware, cups and saucers that can double your space.

• Use a plastic carrying tray to store cleaning supplies. They'll stay organized and also be portable enough to move from room to room. Or as an alternative, use a cardboard soft drink bottle container for this same purpose. They don't last forever, but they're free!

Not only can this baker's rack expand a kitchen's storage quotient, in time of need it can actually become the kitchen itself. In a studio apartment or guest house that isn't equipped with a kitchen, the rack can hold cooking appliances as well as dishes, utensils and linens. A nifty, portable mini-table and stool provides a place to eat in the makeshift kitchen, and can also be used as a butcher's block "island."

When floor and counter space is lacking in the kitchen, the walls can offer a good alternative for storage of cooking-related miscellany. There are lots of different types of racks and knobs available for purchase, or you can make your own pieces to hang linens, utensils, etc. from walls and cupboards.

An expandable rack painted to match the collection of teacups adds instant decor to a kitchen wall. This rack can also be used for utensils, potholders or small appliances.

Three of the hangers shown were purchased or put together through pieces found at a home improvement store. The same wooden rack base is embellished three different ways in these photos.

We added drawer handles to the vertical rack (top left) pewter drawer pulls to the rack at left and decorative fabric and coat hooks to the hanger at right. (Instructions on page 83.)

• Store utensils in either the first or last place you're going to use them.

• Keep the most often used utensils near the stove, such as wooden spoons, colanders, pots and pans and spatulas. There are many containers that are not only functional but also attractive, such as terra-cotta pots, unique jars or baskets.

• Keep the utensils that aren't used as often in the drawer, organized with drawer dividers. There are  many to choose from, including expandable ones to fit in most size drawers. You can also purchase plastic strips that can be used to create your own divider system.

• If possible, try installing the microwave on a wall to free up valuable counter space.

• Store brooms, mops and dustpans on a wall-mounted rack on the back of the broom closet door. This frees up space for other things to be stored such as pet supplies.

• Keep waste baskets off the kitchen floor by converting a kitchen cupboard to hold a sliding waste container.

• Store baking pans on the back of cupboard doors with the use of magnets. Purchase large, round heavy-duty magnets at the hardware store and glue them to the cupboard door. When put away, the baking pans will stick to the magnets. If using aluminum pans (which are not magnetic), place a loose magnet inside the pan and attach the pan to the cupboard door magnet.

• Use walls or ceiling to hang pots and pans. This will free up needed cupboard space for other uses. Use hanging pan racks or wall mounted racks for decorative pots and pans display and storage.

• For an inexpensive, yet effective wine rack, use an old cardboard carpet roll (find them at your local flooring store). Cut them to the length of wine bottles. Either paint the rolls or cover them with attractive self-adhesive shelf paper. Glue the rolls together using industrial strength glue. Insert bottles in openings.

• If you don't have a wine cellar, you should store your wine in the bottom of a hall closet which will keep the wine at a constant temperature.

CHAPTER THREE

BEDROOMS & CLOSETS

BEDROOMS & CLOSETS

The most personal place in the house is your bedroom. It's in this sanctuary that you go to escape the day's pressures, to relax and to rest. It's important how the room is arranged and decorated. If your room is small, you'll need to do some careful planning to make your daily routine run smoothly.

• Choose bedside tables carefully. You'll want one or two with enough space on top for a lamp, clock, phone and tissues and with open shelves for books, magazines and phone book. A drawer in the table can hold your private journal, pens and notepads, toiletries and medications.

• Daybeds are a wonderful invention for small bedrooms or studio apartments with no bedroom at all. The bed can be made up to serve as a couch during the day and then as a bed at night. A collection of decorator pillows can make the daybed look like a stylish sofa.

• You might want your bedroom to double as a home office, so you're going to have to plan a space for a desk and chair. A folding screen is useful for dividing your bedroom if you're also using it as a home office (see page 71).

• Do you need more space for your overflowing supply of books? Try adding some free standing bookshelves against one wall in your room to solve that problem.

• Sometimes placing the bed at an angle can provide more space in the room. Experiment with your furniture arrangement to see how you can maximize your space.

A recessed alcove has great "small space" potential, useable in so many ways. In this master bedroom, the niche's three walls are lined with floor-to-ceiling curtains to envelop a set of chairs. The addition of a round table makes this a perfect spot to relax and enjoy coffee and the Sunday paper. This colorful sitting area also becomes a wonderful decorative focal point for the room.

A small alcove with a window like the one above is the the perfect place for a window seat. In a small bedroom, a window seat provides extra seating and a cozy spot to read and relax.

Life in a studio apartment doesn't have to mean a sleeper sofa and bean bag chairs. This studio is lushly decorated, and includes both a bed and a sofa. The unique arrangement has the sofa flush against the end of the bed with a coffee table placed in front. The cozy look works for the rectangular room and makes a boldly original decorative statement, too. Note the wonderful coordination of color and pattern in the window treatments, bedding and throw pillows.

SMALL SPACE SOLUTIONS

• If there's no space for a television, one can be placed on a cart with wheels which can be stored in a closet and rolled out when needed.

• For more storage, a trunk at the foot of the bed provides much needed space for extra linens.

• Storage boxes with out-of-season clothing can be easily stored under a bed.

Got a bedroom without a closet? Your local home improvement store has just what you need—a handy "closet on wheels."

This canvas cover keeps your clothing and accessories under wraps and has many decorative possibilities. As shown, it's been stamped in a gold, fleur-de-lis pattern, then crowned with a regal vestment. Golden tassels, braid trim and gold closure buttons complete the cover. Now it's a striking conversation piece. (Instructions on page 84).

A hanging peg rack offers another place to keep accessories, such as necklaces and scarves, without using up precious floor space. This wooden example has pretty, carved scrollwork, so it doubles as an attractive wall decoration for the bedroom.

An organized closet doesn't have to be made up entirely of metal and wood laminate structures. The newest, softer clutter-reducers are hanging drawers and stackable cubes made with pretty fabrics, and include dozens of cubbies for shoes, slippers, mittens, etc. Lidded boxes come in a variety of shapes, sizes and colors to hold clothes, accessories...whatever you like to keep tucked away in the bedroom. The right organizers will greatly expand the storage capacity of your closet, and the mix and match patterns and containers let this space be your pride and joy.

CLOSETS

Having an organized closet in your bedroom can make all the difference in your busy life. It's time to purge those old clothes, shoes, coats and accessories that are no longer in fashion. Here's some ideas for organizing your closet:

• Hang coat hangers with their hooks pointing away from you. This makes removing clothing easier especially if you need to move several articles at once.

• If you hang all of your short things in one area of the closet, you'll create room for either another rod, a shoe rack or small dresser.

• If your hangers don't slide easily on a wooden rod, try rubbing a little paste furniture wax over it.

• So that you won't have to search for a hanger, always place the empties at the end of the rod.

• Too dark in your closet? Add a battery-operated unit to the closet ceiling.

• When you notice sets of plastic hangers on sale, buy a bunch. You can never have enough.

• If you can afford it, hire a professional to redo your closets. They'll measure your closet, interview you about your wants and desires, then present you with a plan. They'll totally reorganize your closet either with built-in cabinets or wooden shelves, wire basket drawers and additional rods.

• If you can't afford the professionals, try reorganizing your own closet. There are many systems available at home improvement centers and storage and discount chain stores to help you create your own custom closet.

This wardrobe organizer doesn't take a lot of wall space, and creates a closet where there once was none. Stackable wire baskets and fabric hanging compartments store his shoes, socks, clothes, towels and bedding in style. A horizontal pole suspends a cloth hamper and other clothing. There's extra storage room above and in the lower level bins and buckets. An added curtain makes it easy to hide belongings when entertaining guests.

CHAPTER FOUR

BATHROOMS

BATHROOM SPACE-SAVING IDEAS

The bathroom is usually the smallest room in the house. But so many things need to be stored there. Here's some ideas for gaining more space:

• Consider adding additional cabinets—either built-ins (if this is affordable) or freestanding cabinets which are usually very affordable. There are many different sizes and types available.

• Or make existing cabinets more efficient by adding such things as back-of-the-door racks, lazy susans, or pull-out drawers. Use divider trays to store small essentials in bathroom drawers.

• Look for forgotten spaces in the bathroom that might be of use, such as the space above a toilet. There are many shelving units available for this space. Or you could add your own simple shelves to the above-the-toilet space. Glass shelves will give a feeling of spaciousness and look very attractive with perfume bottles and other toiletries, not to mention small plants, candles and other small decorator items.

• Space above the door can be utilized for linen storage just by adding a simple shelf.

• If there's no available wall space in a tiny bathroom, consider storing towels and other linens in a basket that can fit in the empty space between the tub and toilet.

• Use a see-through shower curtain in a tiny bathroom to make the room appear larger.

• Look for under-the-counter baskets (usually used in kitchen cabinets) to hold small appliances and other bathroom items.

• To keep used towels off the floor, keep a hamper in the bathroom. One might fit in a cabinet, or a corner (corner hampers are available for just this purpose). If there's no floor space available, but a little bit of wall space, hang a fabric hamper with drawstring on a peg.

• The tall, narrow cabinet pictured on page 39 can hold a multitude of bathroom supplies and takes up very little space. Store towels, washcloths, soaps, shampoos, miscellaneous toiletries, hair dryers, curling irons, shavers, and first aid items.

• A cloth shoe organizer can be put into service on the back of a bathroom door to hold many small appliances and toiletries, as well as magazines, small books, and soaps. You might want to use the vinyl variety in the bathroom because it will be easier to clean.

• Shower caddies can be used hung on a wall to hold various bathroom items.

• Cup hooks can come in handy in the bathroom. Screw them in under shelves to hang small appliances such as hair dryers, electric curlers or shavers. The more you keep off your counter, the neater your bathroom will be.

• An easy decorating tip for the bathroom that doesn't entail redecorating, is to have several sets of towels on hand in different colors. When you change the towels, you change the whole mood of the room. Change towels often and see what a difference it makes.

The versatile baker's rack shown on page 23, is just as handy in the bathroom, with plenty of space to store towels, toiletries, and paper products. Great for a bathroom that lacks storage or a home with minimal linen-closet space, it can also be placed in a nearby bedroom or hallway. Note how the colorful wicker baskets coordinate with towels and decorative accents. It's true...organization can be beautiful.

A trio of shiny, metallic paint cans work nicely to hold guest towels on the bathroom countertop. Different sized cans can be glued together to make a set, then stuffed with rolled up towels for a unique display. (Instructions on page 84)

Filled with rolled up hand towels, a hanging tin planter is a charming surprise in a tiny powder room. It takes up very little width space on a peg or nail, or hang it from a small, hooked wall shelf, as shown. The shelf adds a bit of extra storage for toiletries.

Free up bathroom walls to make room for a long mirror or artwork by confining towels to unused countertop space. A wire, multi-pot plant stand is a pretty way to hang a lot of towels in a small area. The addition of a matching ceramic pot gives it real decorative panache. Insert a plant in the pot or use it to hold soaps and lotions.

The drawer divider usually used in a kitchen can also become a handy space-saver in the bath. Filled with small toiletries, beauty supplies and cosmetics, it can be tucked into a narrow drawer to keep clutter from bathroom counters.

A very small bathroom doesn't have the floor space to accommodate most storage units, but think vertically and you can pack a lot of shelving into a tiny area. This tall, narrow unit is perfect for an undersized room. Its seven compartments hold and organize towels, paper goods and toiletries, freeing the under sink area for cleaning supplies and medicinal items.

These modular cubes are so versatile, you might want to take advantage of their storage potential in several rooms! Here, they're stacked into a vertical tower, utilizing less than two square feet of floor space to triple the storage provisions in this bathroom. The open square at bottom can keep a small trash receptacle or basket full of paper goods, while drawers hold cosmetics or medicines. The divided cube displays an assortment of colorful rolled towels, and the top shelf shows off a decorative planter.

Maybe there isn't a countertop or drawer in sight, but even the tiniest of bathrooms has useable wall space. Hung on the wall, a small cabinet like this is charming and can hold perfume bottles, bath supplies and cosmetics. It can substitute for a missing medicine chest.

CHAPTER FIVE

BABY'S ROOM

BABY'S ROOM

Luckily, babies don't require a whole lot of space. The nursery should include a place to sleep, a little storage room, a place to change diapers, a chair, a lamp and a night-light.

• No matter how small the room, you'll want to decorate it with paint or wallpaper, soft cozy furnishings and lots of cute accessories.

• Look for a changing table that will double as handy storage. A table with two or more shelves can hold diapers, towels, wipes, toiletries, tee-shirts and night-gowns.

• A small dresser can hold every-thing else the baby will need including clothing, socks, bootees, receiving blankets, even some soft toys and books.

• A small closet can be organized to store all of baby's necessities. See page 43 for an example of a well-organized closet. This can easily be achieved using readily available storage organizers. The storage accessories can be temporary. When baby grows up, the closet can be redesigned as desired.

• Keep safety in mind when planning the nursery. Use safety gates, cribs that conform to regula-tions, smoke alarms, saftey covers for electrical outlets, safety locks for windows and doors.

• If you're going to be sharing your bedroom with baby, you might add a folding screen between the areas which will give a sense of privacy and also screen off any clutter or mess.

If baby's nursery is limited to the space taken up by a crib, smart decorative techniques help you make the most of the room you have. This coordinated ensemble utilizes the wall space to create the sense of a 'nursery nook.' A canopy cascades from a dramatic, ceiling-high valance, encompassing the crib in a gauzy curtain border. The matching dust ruffle creates a covered storage area for baby supplies under the crib.

When the crib is outgrown, remove the front bars and you'll have a charming day bed, the perfect place for a child to curl up with a book.

A small armoire, such as this antique, adds decorative warmth and substance to a baby and child's room, and is a storage treasure as well. It's got plenty of room for ornamental objects on top, and offers cupboard space for clothing, blankets and toys. Stacked hatboxes can hold accessories and add to the old fashioned feel, as does a vintage christening gown.

Hanging organizers in three different sizes turn a nursery closet into an orderly dream. The entire inventory of shoes, blankets, clothing and accessories can be seen at a glance when the closet door is open, yet all are neatly hidden away when it's shut. These cloth cubes come in many pastel colors, so you can find a perfect match for your nursery décor.

This storage cube works wonderfully for baby items, holding rolled up blankets, towels and onesies. The unique, triangular-shaped compartments filled with a combination of colorful receiving blankets, towels and washcloths makes this solution as cute as it is functional.

It may be tough to get a wide dresser in baby's wee nursery, but you can combine narrow modular pieces to get the storage you need. A three-shelf unit with wicker baskets holds receiving blankets, linens and sleepers, while another offers mini-drawers to store tees and other small clothes and accessories. The canvas drawers come in a rainbow of colors, and we added cute felt numerals and ribbon drawer-pulls for charm. (Number patterns on pages 92–95. Instructions on page 86.)

A purely decorative touch is pretty gingham ribbon running through the metal gridwork to soften the look. Ribbon is also tied to the grid to hang pictures and amusements for baby.

The same baker's rack used in the kitchen (pages 24 and 26) and master bath (page 37) is transformed here into a perfect changing table for baby. Placed in a bathroom or in the nursery, this rack provides for lots of storage and adds color and whimsy too. Additions to the rack are a changing pad, fabric skirting and pastel, organizer baskets. A wooden shelf full of toiletries hangs on the wall within the frame of the unit to complete this tidy set up. (Instructions for the fabric skirt on page 85.)

The skirt easily pulls away to provide easy access to the baskets of baby supplies.

before

Just because a baby's room is tiny (like this add-on room, formerly a porch) doesn't mean it can't pack a lot of pizzazz. The right decorating techniques make the most of the small area, creating a more spacious feel while maintaining the coziness inherent in a small room. Graduated paint shades and a colorful window valance draw the eye up and away from these close set walls. A low table and a toy chest/bench help organize toys and get them off the ground. The cushioned bench top provides seating and a little "book nook." The fabrics coordinate with the crib and valance for a finished look.

after

Rattan storage baskets are put to good use in the nursery here, filling storage cubbies in a unique changing table. Though narrower than most changing tables, this space saver offers plenty of storage-ability. The larger baskets can hold outfits, diapers and linens, while the smaller tabletop duo stores lotions, powders and wipes. (Instructions for the changing pad on page 84.)

A gathered, multi-fabric skirt beautifies this changing table and works to hide the clutter of diapers and supplies on the shelves. This is a way to add fabric and color to a very small nursery where you might not have many decorative furnishing options. (Instructions for the changing table skirt on page 85.)

The white toy chest featuring a blue floral cushion is a comfy spot for curling up and reading a good book. Children's book illustrations are decoupaged to the front and sides of the toy chest for a sweetly charming effect. The lid of the chest lifts up to provide storage for extra toys, books and secret treasures.

You can buy stuffed animal organizers, but it's easy and inexpensive to make your own! Colorful plastic chains can be purchased by the yard. We used self-gripping Velcro straps to secure the pets to the chain. Hung from the ceiling, a furry collection doesn't clutter the floor and becomes part of the room's décor.

CHAPTER SIX

KID'S ROOMS

KID'S ROOMS

Children's rooms have to perform a lot of functions. They have to be a space for playing with friends, a place to explore new interests, display their possessions, have make-believe time and make a mess. The room also is the place for rest and sleep. It's one of the most difficult rooms to organize because of the amount of toys, stuffed animals, doll parts, and books that need to be put away. How do you incorporate all of these activities in one small space?

Luckily there's an endless supply of storage options available. Once you've got the storage units figured out, organization will surely follow. And once you have the kids trained to put their things away, you'll have your problem solved.

1. Start by figuring out the storage that you need. First, sort all of your children's toys by size and shape. When this is done, figure the storage items you'll need:

Bookcases or shelves
Storage containers
Flat boxes for storage under the bed
Labels for all containers
Behind-the-door hangers
Toy chain for stuffed animals
Peg racks for clothing, hats and scarves
Baskets for additional toy storage

2. Now it's time to shop for the storage items that you need.

3. Make a game of putting everything in its new place. In this way the children will know what goes where and be more apt to put their things away later.

4. The closets in a child's room can be made into an organized storage system. Hanging two rods helps to increase space. If the closet is big enough, put a dresser in it to help free up valuable play space. If you don't have a dresser, hanging storage (as pictured on page 43) is great for shirts, undies, socks and nighties.

5. Recyle toys and books from time to time. Let the child know that their decision to donate their old toys will help a disadvantaged child. You'll be killing two birds with one stone—decreasing clutter and teaching the child a wonderful life's lesson.

Labeling of the storage containers is very important and it can also be creative. Shown in a baby's room on page 44, this narrow storage cube features drawers which have been decorated with felt numbers. This is a nice system for letting kids know what toy goes where and also gets them to start learning their numbers.

OTHER LABELING IDEAS:

• Use shipping labels or self-adhesive labels and alphabet stamps to spell the contents.

• Apply fun stickers to the labels that correspond to what's in the container.

• Decorate each label with a magazine picture that gives a hint of the drawer or container's contents. This is a great idea for pre-schoolers who don't read yet.

These multipurpose storage cubes are a natural fit for a child's room, holding baskets and boxes full of toys, books, collections, etc. This example shows the addition of a cushion placed across two cubes, an easy way to create a cozy seating area or faux window seat. The cushion is covered in bright fabric, coordinating with the lampshade for a cute decorative accent. (Instructions for the cushion and lampshade on page 87.)

If a child's bedroom lacks floor space, sometimes the best way to go is up. A loft bed leaves an ample section underneath to use for play, sleeping bag camp-outs or toy storage. Some loft beds come with attachable curtains to cover up the area below, or you can make your own. This model is equipped with a fun slide and sidecar tent, so the bed turns this small dwelling into a combination bed/playroom.

A trundle bed is an ideal way to accommodate kids' overnight friends, but if storage is the more important issue, consider buying one without the mattress. The empty trundle pull-out can be stuffed with extra linens, toys or seasonal clothing, all easily accessible, yet out of sight under the bed. An unused mattress in another room can always be inserted for a sleepover.

Attached to a wall or bedroom door, compartmentalized organizers are a great way to store a lot of little things without taking up floor space. Filled with colorful toys, this fabric shoe holder becomes part of the whimsical décor in a child's room. You can add to the fun by stamping some of the compartments with designs to go with the room's theme. These organizers can also hold baby things or a teen's fashion accessories. (Instructions are on page 86.)

This girl's room is quite small, without enough space for a complete set of traditional bedroom furniture. In these cases, there's no reason a homework desk and small dresser can't take the place of bedside nightstands, holding reading lamps and whatever she needs within easy reach. All the furniture placed along one wall leaves the remainder of the room open for roaming. With no floor space available for décor, walls take the spotlight here, displaying pictures, shelves and other hanging accents to round out the garden theme.

SMALL SPACE DECORATOR TIPS

• Just because a room is small doesn't mean it can't be beautifully decorated. Choose a theme that your child would like, such as the garden theme pictured here and carry it thoughout the room.

• A bulletin board covered in fabric and criss-crossed ribbon can neatly display homework assignments, birthday cards, concert tickets and other mementos.

• Brightly painted wire baskets in different shapes and sizes can be mounted above the desk to hold favorite photographs, school supplies, art projects, CDs and magazines.

Create a day bed effect from a single bed by pushing it into a corner and adding extra throw pillows. This lets a boy and his friends sit comfortably in the room, no matter its small size. The nightstand shown has three tiers, so it offers extra space for books and magazines. This is the perfect space for him to lounge while doing homework. The next page shows a more feminine version of this same room arrangement.

The placement of this single bed helps transform it into a lovely day bed, a place to slumber by night and sit and talk with friends by day. An application of wallpaper and chair railing in the corner, coordinating with the pillows and dust ruffle, adds to the illusion of a lovely, versatile "living room" in addition to a bedroom.

If the bed and dresser leave only a small corner free in a child's room, consider a miniature table and chairs as a versatile purchase. There's plenty of play value here, whether she's throwing tea parties, playing board games or creating art work. The table also provides a handy space for doing homework.

The tea party theme of the table and chairs is carried out in the wall art seen at right. The Victorian-inspired shelf displays a treasured tea set.

For a boy's room, a more tailored shelf could display his collection of miniature cars or trains.

CHAPTER SEVEN

DORM ROOMS

There are all kinds of rules about what you can or cannot do in a dorm room. Each school is different, so check with them before you go out and purchase paints, wallpapers, or shelves only to find out that these things are not allowed. Most schools don't allow paint or nails on the walls. But this doesn't mean you can't decorate.

• Try blowing up a favorite black and white photo (of a girlfriend, boyfriend, favorite star, pet) and colorize several versions "ala Andy Warhol" either using a computer or just colored markers. With poster hanging adhesive or pushpins hang these photos on the wall in a grouping.

• Hang large sheets of butcher paper or blank newspaper print on the wall using the removable adhesive. Use it to write yourself notes (make sure the markers you use don't seep through the paper and mark the walls), add phone numbers or have friends add their artistic touches when they come to visit. Before you know it, you'll have a wonderful piece of artwork on the wall.

• A small dorm room can be dressed up with the addition of small throw rugs. You can find real bargains at your local discount store, or purchase remnants from a carpet store. Not only will this help decorate the room, but it also adds a touch of warmth.

• Add touches of fabric to soften the room. How about covering a chair with a beautiful floral print or a handsome stripe. There are sewing patterns available for covering every type of chair imaginable. Have Mom or Grandma whip one up for you and ship it in your next care package. Or purchase inexpensive seat covers to hide any spills or stains on your dorm room chair.

• A soft chenille throw gracefully placed over a worn chair definitely makes a decorator statement.

• For an easy and inexpensive change of bedcoverings, cut a length of fleece, fringe the edges and use it to cover your bed. Fleece is available in 60" widths and doesn't require hemming. This fun and functional fabric comes in wonderful new bright colors and prints. See the instructions for making no-sew fleece pillows and throws on page 63.

• If you're not allowed to have real plants in your room, try purchasing the silk variety. There's nothing like a little greenery to spruce up the place. Or try an arrangement of silk flowers. The one's available now are so lifelike, no one will believe you didn't just purchase them from the florist. No place for plants or flowers? Try hanging a basket of greenery from the ceiling (if that's allowed). Or a series of vases with one bud each set on a windowsill adds color and nature to any room.

• If you're not allowed to hang shelves for extra storage, use narrow boxes under the bed. There are bed risers available that can elevate the bed a few inches so that you can store much more under there.

• Make your own bookcases using the old cinder block and boards idea. Not only will they be functional, but inexpensive as well.

• If you're sharing a room and want a little more privacy, add a folding screen between beds.

A loft bed with a modular work station below could be the perfect solution for a student in cramped quarters. These pieces include a desk and chair along with shelves and a cupboard for supplies. Stacked photo storage boxes help keep classwork projects organized and clutter to a minimum. This set up would work in a dorm room (where allowed), studio apartment or in a home office.

Made of denim, this room divider is less expensive than
wooden screens and comes with handy storage pockets, too.
It's a perfect way to obtain some privacy in a dorm room, or
separate a section of a studio apartment. With glued-on vinyl
fronts on many of the pockets, this divider can double as a
display unit, too. Color photos and magazine cut-outs
personalize the screen and help decorate the room.
(Instructions on page 88.)

Just like any other futon, this home-made model provides extra seating in a room, then opens up to make into a bed for a guest. The difference is, it's made with custom-selected fabric to suit the tastes of a college-bound student. (Instructions on page 88.) A multi-cubby storage piece is also put to creative use here, keeping magazines and catalogs handy.

The futon is dressed for a nighttime snooze with a soft fringed fleece throw and fluffy pillows. (Instructions for the no-sew fleece throw and pillows on page 90.)

Cement blocks layered with wooden boards can make a great storage unit and the cost is very minimal. These boards, purchased from a home improvement store were already painted black and now this offbeat bookcase is a "cool" look for a dormitory or teen's room. The cement blocks even come with their own cubbies, places to stash pens and other small items that can clutter up a student's room.

No dorm room should be without flexible storage cubes, which can be placed beside a bed to double as a nightstand. This stacked, four-piece basic holds lots of student necessities along with a lamp for reading. The drawers are decorated with removable stickers, adding colorful stripes to coordinate with bedding. Wooden appliques can also be used to dress up the fronts of these drawers.

The rules at many college dormitories say no nails may be used on the walls, but bare walls can be a bit, well, boring! This table runner is a perfect, decorative way to display photos, cards and mementos, which slip easily into the bamboo slats. Hang the runner using heavy-duty double-sided tape or pushpins. Available at import stores, these runners can also be used as hanging dividers when friends share a room.

CHAPTER EIGHT

HOME OFFICES & CRAFT ROOMS

CRAFT ROOMS

No matter what type of craft you are involved in whether it's knitting, cross stitch, scrapbooking, weaving or rubber stamping, if you don't get your space organized it will be difficult to finish your projects. You don't need a lot of space to get organized, just a bit of planning and creativity. It would be nice to have a separate room for these activities because crafting can certainly produce clutter! But if space is limited, you might have to convert an unused closet to a craft area, or a spot in the garage or attic. A laundry room can sometimes double as a sewing area because it contains the necessary ironing board.

Some kitchen organizers can find their way into a craft area. Here the  expandable organizer shelf commonly used in the kitchen for spice storage is used to store and display rubber stamps. This handy tiered shelf can also hold an assortment of paints to make them easy to reach.

Another kitchen organizer that can come in handy in a craft room is the versatile lazy susan. This revolving organizer can hold a collection of rubber stamps which are clearly visible from all angles. The lazy susan with a  container in the center not only holds an assortment of acrylic paints, but also a selection of paintbrushes.

One visit to a craft or fabric store will provide a multitude of ideas and products for getting your craft area organized. You'll find baskets, plastic containers, tubs, racks, rolling suitcases, and every other kind of tool to get your hobby organized. You'll find more storage ideas at home improvement centers and discount chain stores. 99 cent stores also carry a large selection of stackable storage containers.

The storage cubes pictured at right can be used in lots of different ways to store craft supplies.

This modular storage solution is a wonderful asset for a sewing, craft or hobby room. The divided cubes are ideal spots for skeins of yarn, while the open shelves contain crochet threads begging to be made into a warm, cozy afghan. Embroidery floss kept in handy plastic containers fit neatly into the upper shelf. The storage basket holds works in progress, and the drawers are full of sewing notions, cross stitch fabric and other needlework essentials.

A wooden shoe rack, used for wine storage on page 22, can also hold skeins of yarn. Each is readily visible and easy to reach, and together they create a colorful display for the craft room.

HOME OFFICES

It would be nice to have a separate room for your office. But if space is limited, you might choose a corner that will work just fine. This is an ideal place to set up a divider to separate you from the rest of the house. This office will probably be for your eyes only, but since it's part of your home, it should be organized and free of clutter. If you plan this space just right, it can be your office during the day and part of a living room, dining room or den at night.

• When you choose the area, make sure there is enough space for a desk and your other equiment such as your computer and printer. It's also essential that an elecrical outlet is nearby and a telephone jack.

• If you don't have a real desk, consider using alternatives. A hollow door placed atop two filing cabinets would work just fine and also provide storage for your paperwork.

• There are also wonderful computer stations available that can house all your equipment, paperwork and even a CD player and collection of CDs.

• An armoire style computer desk is ideal because when the work day is over, you can just close the doors and your office area becomes a handsome piece of furniture.

• Hang a wooden window box next to a desk and fill it with flower pots. Fill the pots with pens, pencils, rulers, scissors and other handy tools.

If your home office is part of your living room or bedroom, consider using a screen divider to separate the two areas. A solid screen lends a feeling of privacy to the desk area and hides paperwork clutter from the bedroom. These types of folding screens come in fabric and metal also, but wood gives this piece furniture-quality status.

If you don't have a designated room to use as a home office, you may be able to find a nook or alcove that will fit a desk and chair. Here, the landing area at the top of a staircase is put to good use, and just accommodates a computer work station. The sunny window makes this a pleasant place for kids to do homework or for adult business and other pursuits.

If a small bedroom doesn't have room for both a nightstand and a desk, why not let a desk double as a nightstand? A narrow desk can fit into the space between the wall and bed, and hold a reading lamp, phone and decorative items. Along with other desk supplies, the drawers might hold magazines, tissue and a cache of unread novels.

Dress up a sewing room with fancy storage. The clothes hamper (from page 17) is used here as a table/storage unit. It's just the right size to hold sewing supplies. In addition, the empty space inside offers storage potential for finished projects or prized antique quilts (at right). In a home office or hobby room, this hamper can be used to store a number of other things, from gift wrap paraphenalia to rolls of handmade papers. The stylish stacked hat boxes can store scraps of fabric and other sewing tools for the avid quilter. Even though your craft room or area may be small, it still deserves to be decorated. Here an antique quilt and braided rug help beautify and define this space.

Chic, yet shabby, these cast-off file drawers can be very useful, especially if your home office desk is lacking drawer space of its own. Loose drawers can sit along the back of the desktop, keeping files and reading material organized and close at hand. These drawers were removed from a broken chest, and their weathered appearance adds rustic ambience to antique-theme decor.

Inexpensive photo storage boxes can be used in many ways in your home office, organizing bills, correspondence and tax receipts. They come in a variety of colors and prints, and can be attractively stacked on a desk or even on the floor in a corner. These boxes would also fit nicely into modular storage cubes (shown on page 68).

There is no end to the ways you can put drawer organizing inserts to work in your home. Most popularly, these are used in the kitchen to keep flatware and cooking tools separate, but they're equally at home in bathrooms, bedrooms, hobby rooms, offices and garages. This two-tiered, plastic model boasts compartments to organize art supplies, homework helpers, a set of woman's tools, and sewing notions. Wherever you have a storage drawer in your home, you can reduce clutter and make things easier to find with one of these versatile organizers.

CHAPTER NINE

HALLWAYS & GARAGES

HALLWAYS

THE HALL CLOSET

Hallways are sometimes a forgotten space in a house. But if you live in a really small space, the hallway can become a space-efficient storage area such as the one at right.

A hallway usually does not receive any decorative consideration. It should have a welcoming feel and serve as an introduction to the house. If you're using it for storage, you'll want the shelves and racks to be attractive.

• Look also for "dead" spaces such as under stairways and stair landings. These can provide valuable storage as well.

• You can maximize the sense of space in a hallway by adding recessed shelves and mirrors.

• A peg rack hung all along a hallway provides a place for hats, scarves, backpacks, umbrellas and even the dog's leash.

• For boots and extra shoes that don't fit into the closets, add a cabinet in the hall. Place a narrow bench nearby for changing shoes when you're coming and going.

• A hallway can provide much needed wall space to hang extra artwork that doesn't fit in the rest of the house. This not only solves the problem of where to hang the extra pictures, but also adds to the beauty of the hallway.

• A small table near the front door is an excellent place for leaving messages and for collecting the mail. Place a basket on the table for the mail and go through it often to weed out junk mail and pri-oritize bills and other important mail.

• A bulletin board in the hallway can serve as a handy message center for the whole family.

• A very narrow hallway may have just enough space for hanging shelves. You might want to line the complete hallway from floor to ceiling with shelves to house your paperback book collection.

What's usually in your hall closet? When you open the door does everything come tumbling out?

If your answer is yes, it's time to get that closet organized. Next time you have guests you'll be so happy that you did.

1. Ask yourself what you want your closet to be:

for extra storage?
a guest closet?
a place for kid's things?

2. Examine what's in there now. Take an inventory and decide what stays and what goes.

3. Label four boxes and sort items as follows:

keepers
tossers
donations
garage sale

4. Put items that don't belong in the hall closet in their appropriate places. If you have a mudroom or closet in the back of the house, this is a good place for the kid's coats, boots, scarves and hats. Other items might go on a rolling rack, armoire or hooks (peg racks either in a bedroom or hallway.)

5. Now rearrange your empty closet. Store small items such as scarves and gloves in see-through plastic stackable boxes, hats in stackable hat boxes, kids shoes in stacked milk crates, back packs on peg hooks on the back of the door, umbrellas or canes in tall narrow baskets or hung

on hooks on one wall of the closet. Now the closet is free to hang coats, jackets and maybe some extra out-of-season clothing.

In a large family, or where kids' bedroom space is limited, school and recreational supplies can become a real clutter problem. This organizer unit makes excellent use of one 11 foot-wide wall of space, with not an inch wasted from floor to ceiling. It stores jackets, shoes, sports equipment, backpacks and games, keeping everything off the floor and furniture. The unit, which includes shelves, hanging poles (with shoe organizer) and oversized buckets and boxes, might be placed in a rumpus room, communal hallway, utility room or even the garage.

LAUNDRY ROOM

If you don't live in a house with a separate laundry room, don't despair. There are plenty of odd spaces where a washer and dryer will fit in nicely. Whether your washer and dryer are in a hallway, garage, bedroom or bathroom, you'll want the space to be efficient and organized. Here are some helpful ideas:

• Hang a rod up near the washer and dryer. Extension rods are inexpensive and easy to install. It's handy for hanging drip dry or freshly ironed clothing. If there's no place to hang a rod, use a free-standing clothes rack. Look for one with wheels so that you can move it around when needed.

• A closet can be transformed into a laundry area using a stacking washer and dryer. These only require about five square feet of floor space. Use the back of the closet door to hang racks for laundry supplies.

• To keep clutter down, say this to yourself everytime you do the laundry, "Wash, Dry, Put Away". When you follow these three easy steps, you'll be so happy with your organized drawers and closets when you reach for neatly folded or hung up clothing.

• Keep hampers off the floor by using special cabinet units that slide in and out of a cupboard.

• Hang shelves in the space over the washer and dryer to neatly store cleaning supplies.

Why doesn't every laundry room come equipped with a foldaway ironing-board wall unit? The good news is, this handy, hang-up model, complete with built-in light and space for an iron, can be purchased at your local home improvement store. This is wonderful for a laundry room, or it can be used elsewhere if you don't have a laundry room. It keeps the ironing board off the floor and out of closets, so it's perfect for a small home or apartment.

If you love the look of antiques, don't leave your laundry room out of the picture. The one pictured above is decorated with a vintage sign, decorative jars filled with cleaning essentials and handy baskets holding towels for drying hand-washables.

The hamper pictured on pages 17 and 72 is used here, as originally intended, to hold dirty clothes. If bedrooms are small, this attractive hamper can be placed in the laundry room or even the garage.

GARAGE

Your garage can be your most functional area. It's usually a pretty big room and has wide open spaces and can serve lots of purposes. Right now, your garage might not be empty, or neat or free of clutter. You might not even be able to put your car there! So it's time to get your garage organized

Where to start?

1. The first thing to do is start getting rid of things you don't need anymore. You'll need a supply of trash bags and three big boxes. Sort the items into four piles:

keep
donate
garage sale
trash

2. When you've finished this daunting task, it's time to do something with the things you're going to keep. Sort these items into the following categories (you might want to add others):

Tools	Others
Garden things	
Holiday items	_____
Paints and brushes	_____
Sports equipment	
Laundry supplies	_____
Cleaning items	_____

3. Now that these things are categorized and in one spot, you can decide how you want to store them and what types of shelves, hooks and storage containers you'll need. Look around your garage and see if you already own some storage items. Then decide what you need to purchase. Check storage catalogs or home improvement centers, discount stores and craft and fabric stores to find storage items that will work for you.

4. You don't have to purchase everything at once. Do one section of the garage at a time. Not only will the job be less daunting, but you won't go broke buying all those storage items at one time.

5. Supply your garage with a variety of hooks for different jobs. These hooks and hangers can contribute to overall organization of your garage. A handy one is the spring clip which holds handles ranging from ¾ to 1¼ inches in diameter. It attaches easily with only one screw. Spring clips are also available mounted on a sliding track or with hooks that attach to pegboard.

6. When you have your storage boxes, tubs and containers—you'll need to label them. Use a large black marker and self-adhesive labels. Write neatly with big letters so that you'll be able to find your things easily.

7. Deal with the trash you've generated.

• Check with your local trash department to see if they have limits on how much you can throw away. Inquire about regulations on picking up large items.

• Order a dumpster if you're doing a major overhaul or if you're moving and need to throw away a lot of trash.

• Local thrift shops will be happy to take your cast-offs that are in good condition. Some will even come and pick up large items.

• The Goodwill, Salvation Army, Amvets and other charitable organizations will also take your unwanted items. Check your yellow pages for these organizations.

In an organized garage, items used only occasionally are kept off the floor, yet within ready reach. This can prove difficult when you have a small garage and an active family! Plenty of wall shelving is a necessity, and innovative, new hanging hooks and poles can help as well. This pole storage system is equipped with brackets to hold many items aloft—bikes and rackets, as well as boxes for balls and other smaller objects. On the wall, amply sized hooks hold folding chairs, skis, hockey sticks and other cumbersome sports accessories.

A FEW ORGANIZATION TIPS FROM AN EXPERT

Jean Richards, an interior designer with over 20 years of experience has generously agreed to share some of her tried and true organizational tips.

Three of Jean's favorite storage items are file folders, Post-it™ notes and Ziplock™ bags. She uses them for everything and encourages her clients to do the same.

Here's how she uses them:

• With file folders, Jean creates a complete filing system. She purchases file folders that come in different colors. Then she designates each color with a category. For instance, yellow folders would contain insurance papers; red—house papers, including maintenance information, clippings from magazines; blue—recipes from magazines or friends. The file folders are filed by category in either file drawers or cardboard or plastic transfer files. Not only does this system decrease the clutter in the house, it also makes things easy to find. Just go to the file that's the proper color and voila! There it is.

• She uses Post-it™ notes if she needs files or storage boxes to be easily changed and re-labeled.

• Since Ziplock™ bags come in lots of different sizes, they are handy for storing various types of things. Jean uses the large 2 or 2½ gallon size for storing extra clothing that doesn't fit in the closet. Folded up sweaters are kept neatly in the bags and since the bags are see-through, it's easy to find what you're looking for. These bags are also great for packing when you travel. Just grab the item you want to take along and put the bag in your suitcase.

• The small 2" x 2" bags can be found in craft stores. These can hold little items such as safety pins, buttons, ends of embroidery floss, other sewing notions, keys, etc. The small bags can also help to separate medications.

• Store complete sheet sets in individual bags. No more searching for the pillowcase that goes with that sheet. You've got them all together. Just grab the bag when you're ready to change the bed, and the set is all there.

• Here's an interesting idea for using bulletin boards. If you don't want to stick a pin through a treasured photograph or piece of your child's artwork, use map pins to stick into the board and then clip a binder clip to the photograph and hang the clip on the pin.

• For garage storage, plan ahead and purchase your boxes in sets of the same sizes. In this way your storage will be neater and the boxes will stack perfectly. Tape up the boxes on all sides so that dust and dirt can't get into them. Turn the tape under on one end to form a tab so that boxes will be easy to open.

GARAGE SALE TIPS

1. Check to see if you need a permit in your town.
2. Separate like items together and price them using self adhesive stickers or price tags.
4. Use very low prices. Remember this is a garage sale and you want to get rid of these things.
5. Place an ad in your local newspaper with date, time, and address.
6. Make signs using big black markers and legible writing. Hang them where allowed.
7. Print circulars and post them on community bulletin boards, laundromats and grocery stores.
8. Use tables to display glassware, small kitchen items, vases and small appliances. Use free standing racks for hanging clothing.
9. Make the last day half-price day.
10. Donate leftovers to local thrift shops, Amvets, Salvation Army or The Goodwill.

INSTRUCTIONS

Vertical towel rack (p. 27)

You'll need:
Purchased wooden rack
White enamel drawer handles
Red spray paint
Sealer

1. Spray the wooden rack with two coats of red paint. When dry, spray with sealer.

2. Drill holes to correspond with the holes in the drawer handles. Attach the handles, evenly spaced on the rack.

Wooden rack with pewter drawer knobs (p. 27)

You'll need:
Purchased wooden rack
3 pewter drawer knobs
Black spray paint
Sealer

1. Spray the wooden rack using the black paint. Two coats may be necessary. When dry, spray with sealer.

2. Drill holes to correspond with the holes in the knobs.

3. Attach the knobs.

Accordion cup rack (p. 27)

You'll need:
Unfinished accordion rack
Blue spray paint
Sealer

1. Spray the rack blue. Two coats may be necessary. When dry, spray with sealer.

2. Hang mugs or other kitchen supplies.

Wooden rack with coat hooks (p. 27)

You'll need:
Purchased wooden rack
3 black coat hooks   Black spray paint
Sealer   Red check fabric
Black gimp trim   Spray adhesive.
Tacky glue

1. Spray the wooden rack with two coats of black paint. When dry, spray with sealer.

2. Measure and cut fabric to fit the top portion of the rack. Spray the back of the fabric with spray adhesive and apply to the rack, smoothing out any wrinkles as you go.

3. Apply a thin line of tacky glue all around the edge of the fabric and border it with the gimp trim.

4. Drill holes to correspond with the holes in the coat hooks. Attach the hooks.

Garment rack cover (p. 32)

You'll need:
Purchased garment rack cover
Black felt
5 yds. gold cord
8 gold tassels
Foam stamp, fleur-de-lis design
Gold paint
Foam brush
Thread
Fabric glue

1. Cut one strip of black felt 35½" x 5" and two strips 17½" x 5". Using the pattern on page 91, cut out eight triangles.

2. Lay the garment cover on a flat surface. Glue the long felt strip along the top of the front section and the smaller pieces along the top of each side section (refer to photo).

3. Position four triangles across the front section and two triangles on each side section. Glue in place along top edge.

4. Glue cording on edges around the triangles and felt strips. Glue or tack tassels to the end of each triangle.

5. Stamp a design of your choice on the cover. We used a fleur-de-lis design and painted the foam stamp with gold acrylic paint using a foam brush. (Practice stamping on a piece of test paper prior to stamping on the cover).

6. Replace the existing buttons with the gold buttons.

Paint can towel holders (p. 38)

You'll need:
3 plain tin paint cans, various sizes
Industrial strength glue

1. Stack the three cans (as pictured above). Glue the bottom two together at the side using industrial strength glue. When dry, glue the third one on top.

2. Use these to store towels and face cloths on a bathroom counter.

Terry cloth changing pad (p. 47)

You'll need:
Large terry cloth towel
Foam padding, 2" thick
Vinyl
Velcro

1. Fold the towel in half lengthwise and sew across the top edge and down the side edge leaving the bottom open.

2. Sew Velcro to each edge of the open end for closure and for ease of laundering.

3. Place a sheet of vinyl over the foam and insert both into the towel opening.

Skirt for baker's rack changing table (p. 45)

You'll need:
Baker's rack with butcher block top
Yellow, blue and pink gingham fabric
Thread to match
Self-adhesive Velcro tape
Velcro tape

1. Measure from the top of the butcher block to the floor for the length of the skirt. Add 2" for hems.

2. For the width, measure the front and sides of the butcher block. To determine the size of each panel, divide the number of panels needed into the total width measurement. This skirt includes four panels. Double the measurement of each panel (for gathering) and add 1". If rack is also to be used as a room divider, include the back measurement.

3. Cut and sew the front and side panels together using ½" seam allowance. Hem the top, bottom and sides of these two pieces.

4. Machine-sew a basting stitch along the top of both pieces. Gather the tops to fit the butcher block.

5. Sew a strip of Velcro around the top of each piece. Glue a strip of Velcro around the butcher block.

6. Attach the two pieces of the skirt to the Velcro so that the opening is in the front of the baker's rack.

Skirt for Changing Table (p. 47)

You'll need:
5 total yards of fabric, 6 different prints were used
Velcro tape
Self-adhesive Velcro

1. Cut 16 strips 10" x 31" using the various prints. (adjust this measurement according to your particular changing table).

2. Sew the first eight strips together. Sew the other eight strips together.

3. Hem the top and bottom and sides of these two pieces.

4. Machine-sew a basting stitch along the tops of both pieces. Gather the tops to fit the table.

5. Sew a strip of Velcro around the top of each piece. Attach the self-adhesive Velcro to the changing table.

6. Attach the two pieces of the skirt to the Velcro so that the opening is in the front.

Decorated toy storage (p. 44)

You'll need:
Lavender and yellow felt or fleece
Yellow and lavender ribbon
Tacky glue

1. Trace and cut out the number patterns on pages 92-95. Place the patterns on the desired felt colors and cut out the inner and outer number pieces.

2. Glue the number in two layers as pictured.

3. The fabric drawers on this particular storage system included leather strips for pulls. We removed them and added the ribbon pulls to create a more color-coordinated look.

Toy organizer (p. 54)

You'll need:
Purchased fabric shoe organizer
Foam stamps: sailboat, anchor, star
Blue acrylic paint
Foam brush

1. Coat the stamp with the blue paint using the foam brush. Practice stamping on a piece of test paper prior to stamping on the organizer itself.

2. Stamp on the pockets of the organizer in the design of your choice (or refer to photo above for sample design placement).

3. Allow to dry before hanging and adding toys.

Window seat cushion (p. 51)

You'll need:
Fabric
6" thick foam
Thread

1. Measure the window seat. Have a piece of foam cut to this measurement at a fabric store or upholstery shop that does custom cutting.

2. For fabric, add 3¼" to cushion measurement on all four sides. Cut two pieces of fabric to this measurement.

3. Pin top and bottom pieces together, right sides facing and raw edges matching. Leave one side open to insert the foam.

4. Using a ½" seam allowance, stitch around three edges. On the open edge, press back seam allowances for handstitching.

5. To box the corners, separate each corner and use your fingers to press seams open. Align one seam on top of the other and pin. From corner point, measure down seamline 3". Mark and draw a line across the corner perpendicular to the matched seams. Stitch along line. Trim corners.

6. Turn cushion right side out and insert foam, working corners of foam well into pillow corners. Pin open edges together and hand-stitch closed.

Fabric covered lampshade (p. 51)

You'll need:
Self-adhesive lampshade
Fabric
Fabric glue

1. The self-adhesive shade includes a cutting pattern. Lay the pattern on the wrong side of the fabric and trace.

2. Cut the fabric and then hand press it to the sticky shade.

3. Spread fabric glue along the overlapping edge of the fabric and press down to secure.

4. To add trim, measure the top and bottom diameters of the lampshade and cut braid or cord to those measurements adding 1". Hot glue the cord to the top and bottom edge of the shade, trim cord, butt up ends and glue to secure.

DECORATOR TIPS
• Hang a mirror across from a window to reflect the light or next to a lamp to brighten up a small, dark room.
• If you don't have a window in a room, hang a mirror and surround it with molding. Your room will have a feeling of depth and openness.
• Another trick when you don't have a window is to hang a wallpaper mural which depicts scenes of forests, lakes or oceans. Look for them at your wallpaper store or home improvement center.

Denim folding screen (p. 62)

You'll need:
Denim folding screen with pockets
Blue-and-white check ribbon, ¼" wide
1 yd. clear vinyl
Tacky glue

1. Cut vinyl into 10" x 10" squares. The pocket size on this screen is 12" x 12".

2. Lay the screen on a flat surface. Center the vinyl squares on the pockets, one at a time.

3. Glue vinyl to the center of pockets along the bottom and side edges, leaving the top open.

4. Cut two pieces of ribbon 10¼" for sides and one 10½" for bottom. Glue ribbon in place, stopping about ½" from corner.

5. Miter corners by cutting ribbon diagonally through overlapping ribbon. Glue ends and allow to dry.

Futon (p. 63)

You'll need:
6 yds. of 54" wide upholstery fabric
Two 6" foam cushions 30" x 36"
Foam chips for headrest
Fabric marker

Seam allowance – ¾"

1. Cut fabric according to the cutting layout and measurements (at bottom of page). Use pattern on page 91 to cut headrest fabric.

2. Mark the fabric as shown on cutting pattern. Mark dots on main piece (A) 2" on either side of hinge line and 2" at the end of each gusset piece (B). Mark hinge lines on fabric (A and C).

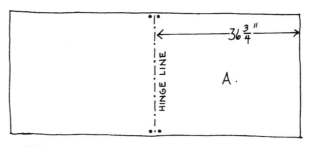

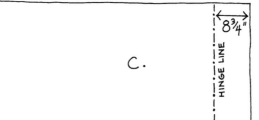

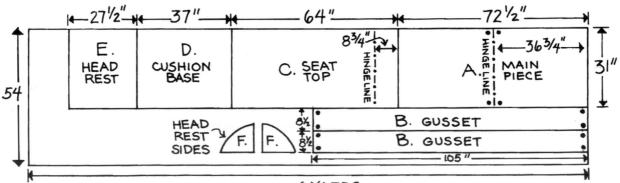

3. Place one headrest piece (F) on headrest top (E) with right sides together matching short edges. Pin and stitch together.

4. Attach the other side of the headrest.

5. Place complete headrest at the opposite end of the hinge line on seat top (C) with right sides together and edges matching as shown. Pin and stitch side edges and outer long edge. Turn headrest right side out. Leave remaining seam open for stuffing.

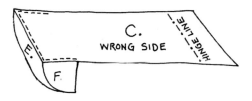

6. With right sides facing, place one short edge of cushion base (D) on opposite end of seat top (C). Pin and stitch together.

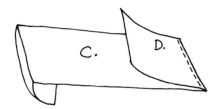

7. Position main piece (A) on seat top (C) and cushion base (D) with right sides facing and hinge lines matching. Pin across to hold in place.

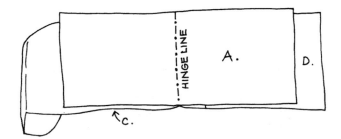

8. With right sides facing, pin one short end of gusset (B) to main piece (A) matching dots at hinge line. Continue pinning down one half of main piece along end and up to dot on opposite side. Stitch in place.

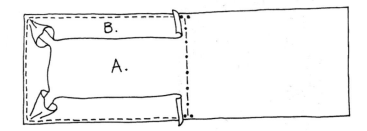

9. Repeat Step 8 with other gusset (B) on the opposite half of the main piece (A).

10. On one side, pin and stitch gusset to seat top (C) again matching dots.

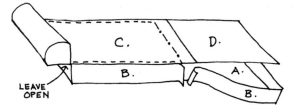

11. Pin and stitch remaining long edge of other gusset to lower front of cushion base (D) leaving back seam open for stuffing.

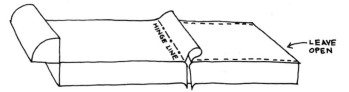

12. Trim seams. Remove pins along hinge line and turn right side out.

(continued on page 90)

13. Match hinge line once again, pin. Clip the seam allowance ⅜" in on both sides of the hinge line.

14. Turn clipped edges under ¾" then top stitch across hinge line. Be sure to clip and turn under seams on both sides of futon.

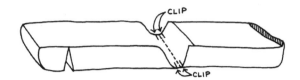

15. Insert foam piece into each cushion section. Turn the open edges ¾" under on cushion base (D). Slip-stitch edges firmly together.

16. Fill the headrest with foam chips. Turn the open edge of the gusset of the seat top (C) under ¾". Overlap this edge over the opening edge of the headrest and pin. Slip-stitch in place firmly.

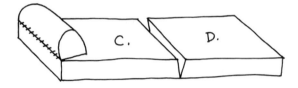

17. To finish the gusset ends of the hinge area, turn the extending fabric under to line up with edge of cushion. Pin and slip-stitch closed.

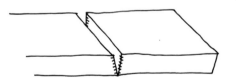

No-sew fleece pillows (p. 63)

You'll need:
½ yd. each turquoise, magenta and lavender fleece
Two 12" pillow forms
One 9" pillow form
Thread to match

1. Cut two each 15" x 15" squares of turquoise and pink fleece and two 12" x 12" squares of lavender fleece.

2. For the fringe, cut in from the edge on all four sides, 3" long and ½" wide strips.

3. Place two squares of like colors together to form top and bottom of pillow.

4. Tie the strips of the pillows together around three sides to form the fringe.

5. Insert pillow form and continue tying the strips on the fourth side to close the pillow.

No-sew fleece throw (p. 63)

You'll need:
3½ yards magenta fleece

1. Cut two pieces of the magenta fleece to measure 56" long and 32" wide.

2. Pin the two pieces together.

3. To form the fringe: lay the throw flat on a cutting table. Cut through both pieces to make fringe. Cut each strip of fringe ½" wide and 4" long. Tie the strips of fringe together around the complete throw.

F

Futon Headrest End
(page 63)

Place fabric right sides
together and cut 2

Enlarge pattern 200%

Garment Rack Cover Pattern
(page 32)

Enlarge pattern 200%

Decorated Toy Storage (page 44)
Outer number patterns

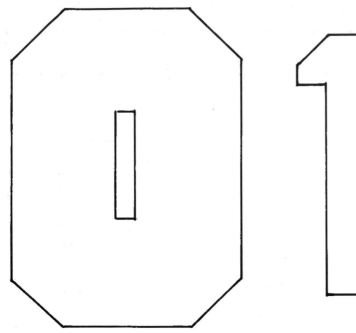 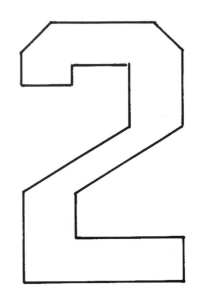

Decorated Toy Storage (page 44)
Inner number patterns

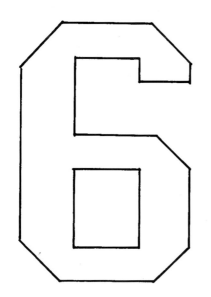 

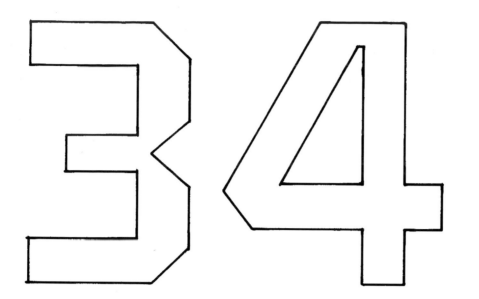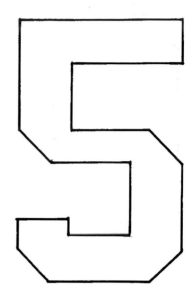

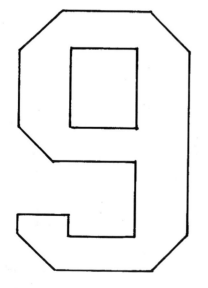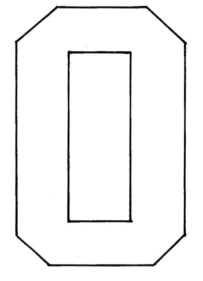

SOURCES

Acrylic Paints & Sealers
Delta Technical Coatings
2550 Pellissier Pl.
Whittier, CA 90601
www.deltacrafts.com

Baskets
Provo Crafts
151 East 3450 North
Spanish Fork, UT 84660
www.provocrafts.com

Furniture
Ikea
www.ikea.com

Ironing Boards
Hide-Away Ironing Boards
5563 South 104th East Ave.
Tulsa, OK 74146
www.hideawayironingboards.com

Yesterday's Garden Basket
119 N. Main Ave.
Fallbrook, CA 92028
www.garden_baskets.com

Projects designed by Jeri Clements and Patsy Needham.

ACKNOWLEDGEMENTS

To Michael Payne, thanks for sharing your dorm room experiences with us. Look for his new book *Let's Ask Michael* for lots more decorating ideas.

We would like to thank Greg Hastings President of Continental Homes in Carlsbad, California for granting us permission to photograph in their beautiful model homes in San Diego County.

Thanks to Julie Wright for allowing us to reprint her dorm room article and photographs and to Corinne Carey, Jayme Ashlock and Jenny Shai for sharing their dorm room ideas with us.

And a special thanks to Brittany Umland and Amy Harbert of Beck Ellman Heald Public Relations and Advertising for their help in supplying us with the Ikea photographs.

Grateful acknowledgement is made to Patsy Needham, Jodi Snyder and Irene Christian for letting us photograph in their "tiny" store, Yesterday's Garden Basket.

PHOTO CREDITS

Julie Wright, pg. 4
Mel Melcon, pg. 8
Patsy Needham, pg. 7 (U)
Hideaway Ironing Boards, pg. 78
Ikea, pg. 14, 17 (BL), 20 (R), 33, 34, 53, 61, 77, 81
Continental Homes, pg. 1, 11, 12, 13, 16, 20 (C), 42, 52, 55-58, 70 and 71

pages Principals:
Barbara Finwall and Nancy Javier
Art Direction: Barbara Finwall
Editorial Direction: Nancy Javier
Photography: Stephen Whalen

Computer Graphic Design: Dana Allison
Computer Graphic Production: Mark Aaron
Project Direction: Jerilyn Clements
Writing: Susan Borsch
Seamstress: Jerilyn Clements

Published by

LEISURE ARTS

LEISURE ARTS
5701 Ranch Drive
Little Rock, AR 72223

© 2003 by Leisure Arts, Inc.

Produced by

pages.

PAGES
P.O. Box 483
Fallbrook, CA 92088